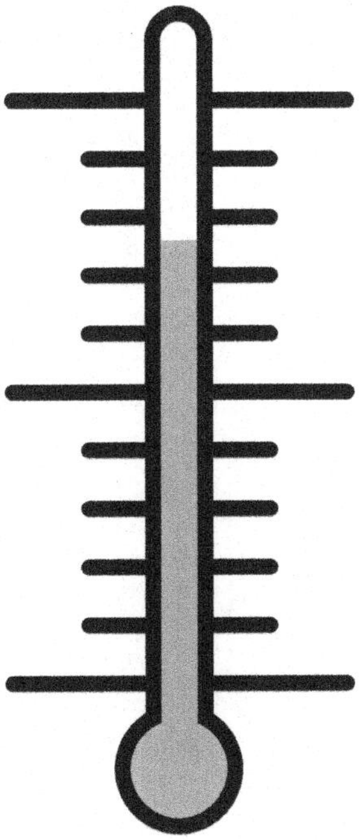

Temperature Log

Name:	
Address:	
Phone:	
Email:	

Temperature Log

Title:	Equipment:
Contents:	
Temp. Range:	

Date	Time	Temp	Notes	Initials

Temperature Log

Title:	Equipment:
Contents:	
Temp. Range:	

Date	Time	Temp	Notes	Initials

Temperature Log

Title:	Equipment:
Contents:	
Temp. Range:	

Date	Time	Temp	Notes	Initials

Temperature Log

Title:	Equipment:
Contents:	
Temp. Range:	

Date	Time	Temp	Notes	Initials

Temperature Log

Title:	Equipment:
Contents:	
Temp. Range:	

Date	Time	Temp	Notes	Initials

Temperature Log

Title:	Equipment:
Contents:	
Temp. Range:	

Date	Time	Temp	Notes	Initials

Temperature Log

Title:	Equipment:
Contents:	
Temp. Range:	

Date	Time	Temp	Notes	Initials

Temperature Log

Title:	Equipment:
Contents:	
Temp. Range:	

Date	Time	Temp	Notes	Initials

Temperature Log

Title:	Equipment:
Contents:	
Temp. Range:	

Date	Time	Temp	Notes	Initials

Temperature Log

Title:	Equipment:
Contents:	
Temp. Range:	

Date	Time	Temp	Notes	Initials

Temperature Log

Title:				Equipment:
Contents:				
Temp. Range:				
Date	Time	Temp	Notes	Initials

Temperature Log

Title:	Equipment:
Contents:	
Temp. Range:	

Date	Time	Temp	Notes	Initials

Temperature Log

Title:	Equipment:
Contents:	
Temp. Range:	

Date	Time	Temp	Notes	Initials

Temperature Log

Title:	Equipment:
Contents:	
Temp. Range:	

Date	Time	Temp	Notes	Initials

Temperature Log

Title:			Equipment:	
Contents:				
Temp. Range:				
Date	Time	Temp	Notes	Initials

Temperature Log

Title:	Equipment:
Contents:	
Temp. Range:	

Date	Time	Temp	Notes	Initials

Temperature Log

Title:	Equipment:

Contents:

Temp. Range:

Date	Time	Temp	Notes	Initials

Temperature Log

Title:			Equipment:	
Contents:				
Temp. Range:				
Date	Time	Temp	Notes	Initials

Temperature Log

Title:	Equipment:
Contents:	
Temp. Range:	

Date	Time	Temp	Notes	Initials

Temperature Log

Title:			Equipment:	
Contents:				
Temp. Range:				
Date	Time	Temp	Notes	Initials

Temperature Log

Title:	Equipment:
Contents:	
Temp. Range:	

Date	Time	Temp	Notes	Initials

Temperature Log

Title:	Equipment:
Contents:	
Temp. Range:	

Date	Time	Temp	Notes	Initials

Temperature Log

Title:			Equipment:	
Contents:				
Temp. Range:				
Date	Time	Temp	Notes	Initials

Temperature Log

Title:	Equipment:
Contents:	
Temp. Range:	

Date	Time	Temp	Notes	Initials

Temperature Log

Title:	Equipment:
Contents:	
Temp. Range:	

Date	Time	Temp	Notes	Initials

Temperature Log

Title:			Equipment:	
Contents:				
Temp. Range:				
Date	Time	Temp	Notes	Initials

Temperature Log

Title:	Equipment:
Contents:	
Temp. Range:	

Date	Time	Temp	Notes	Initials

Temperature Log

Title:	Equipment:
Contents:	
Temp. Range:	

Date	Time	Temp	Notes	Initials

Temperature Log

Title:	Equipment:
Contents:	
Temp. Range:	

Date	Time	Temp	Notes	Initials

Temperature Log

Title:	Equipment:
Contents:	
Temp. Range:	

Date	Time	Temp	Notes	Initials

Temperature Log

Title:	Equipment:

Contents:

Temp. Range:

Date	Time	Temp	Notes	Initials

Temperature Log

Title:	Equipment:
Contents:	
Temp. Range:	

Date	Time	Temp	Notes	Initials

Temperature Log

Title:	Equipment:
Contents:	
Temp. Range:	

Date	Time	Temp	Notes	Initials

Temperature Log

Title:	Equipment:
Contents:	
Temp. Range:	

Date	Time	Temp	Notes	Initials

Temperature Log

Title:	Equipment:
Contents:	
Temp. Range:	

Date	Time	Temp	Notes	Initials

Temperature Log

Title:				Equipment:
Contents:				
Temp. Range:				
Date	Time	Temp	Notes	Initials

Temperature Log

Title:	Equipment:
Contents:	
Temp. Range:	

Date	Time	Temp	Notes	Initials

Temperature Log

Title:	Equipment:
Contents:	
Temp. Range:	

Date	Time	Temp	Notes	Initials

Temperature Log

Title:	Equipment:
Contents:	
Temp. Range:	

Date	Time	Temp	Notes	Initials

Temperature Log

Title:	Equipment:
Contents:	
Temp. Range:	

Date	Time	Temp	Notes	Initials

Temperature Log

Title:	Equipment:
Contents:	
Temp. Range:	

Date	Time	Temp	Notes	Initials

Temperature Log

Title:			Equipment:	
Contents:				
Temp. Range:				
Date	Time	Temp	Notes	Initials

Temperature Log

Title:	Equipment:
Contents:	
Temp. Range:	

Date	Time	Temp	Notes	Initials

Temperature Log

Title:	Equipment:
Contents:	
Temp. Range:	

Date	Time	Temp	Notes	Initials

Temperature Log

Title:	Equipment:
Contents:	
Temp. Range:	

Date	Time	Temp	Notes	Initials

Temperature Log

Title:	Equipment:
Contents:	
Temp. Range:	

Date	Time	Temp	Notes	Initials

Temperature Log

Title:	Equipment:
Contents:	
Temp. Range:	

Date	Time	Temp	Notes	Initials

Temperature Log

Title:				Equipment:
Contents:				
Temp. Range:				
Date	Time	Temp	Notes	Initials

Temperature Log

Title:	Equipment:
Contents:	
Temp. Range:	

Date	Time	Temp	Notes	Initials

Temperature Log

Title:	Equipment:
Contents:	
Temp. Range:	

Date	Time	Temp	Notes	Initials

Temperature Log

Title:	Equipment:
Contents:	
Temp. Range:	

Date	Time	Temp	Notes	Initials

Temperature Log

Title:	Equipment:
Contents:	
Temp. Range:	

Date	Time	Temp	Notes	Initials

Temperature Log

Title:	Equipment:
Contents:	
Temp. Range:	

Date	Time	Temp	Notes	Initials

Temperature Log

Title:	Equipment:
Contents:	
Temp. Range:	

Date	Time	Temp	Notes	Initials

Temperature Log

Title:	Equipment:
Contents:	
Temp. Range:	

Date	Time	Temp	Notes	Initials

Temperature Log

Title:			Equipment:	
Contents:				
Temp. Range:				
Date	Time	Temp	Notes	Initials

Temperature Log

Title:	Equipment:
Contents:	
Temp. Range:	

Date	Time	Temp	Notes	Initials

Temperature Log

Title:	Equipment:
Contents:	
Temp. Range:	

Date	Time	Temp	Notes	Initials

Temperature Log

Title:	Equipment:
Contents:	
Temp. Range:	

Date	Time	Temp	Notes	Initials

Temperature Log

Title:	Equipment:
Contents:	
Temp. Range:	

Date	Time	Temp	Notes	Initials

Temperature Log

Title:	Equipment:
Contents:	
Temp. Range:	

Date	Time	Temp	Notes	Initials

Temperature Log

Title:	Equipment:
Contents:	
Temp. Range:	

Date	Time	Temp	Notes	Initials

Temperature Log

Title:	Equipment:
Contents:	
Temp. Range:	

Date	Time	Temp	Notes	Initials

Temperature Log

Title:			Equipment:	
Contents:				
Temp. Range:				
Date	Time	Temp	Notes	Initials

Temperature Log

Title:	Equipment:
Contents:	
Temp. Range:	

Date	Time	Temp	Notes	Initials

Temperature Log

Title:	Equipment:
Contents:	
Temp. Range:	

Date	Time	Temp	Notes	Initials

Temperature Log

Title:	Equipment:
Contents:	
Temp. Range:	

Date	Time	Temp	Notes	Initials

Temperature Log

Title:	Equipment:
Contents:	
Temp. Range:	

Date	Time	Temp	Notes	Initials

Temperature Log

Title:	Equipment:
Contents:	
Temp. Range:	

Date	Time	Temp	Notes	Initials

Temperature Log

Title:			Equipment:	
Contents:				
Temp. Range:				
Date	Time	Temp	Notes	Initials

Temperature Log

Title:	Equipment:
Contents:	
Temp. Range:	

Date	Time	Temp	Notes	Initials

Temperature Log

Title:	Equipment:
Contents:	
Temp. Range:	

Date	Time	Temp	Notes	Initials

Temperature Log

Title:	Equipment:
Contents:	
Temp. Range:	

Date	Time	Temp	Notes	Initials

Temperature Log

Title:	Equipment:
Contents:	
Temp. Range:	

Date	Time	Temp	Notes	Initials

Temperature Log

Title:	Equipment:
Contents:	
Temp. Range:	

Date	Time	Temp	Notes	Initials

Temperature Log

Title:	Equipment:
Contents:	
Temp. Range:	

Date	Time	Temp	Notes	Initials

Temperature Log

Title:	Equipment:
Contents:	
Temp. Range:	

Date	Time	Temp	Notes	Initials

Temperature Log

Title:	Equipment:
Contents:	
Temp. Range:	

Date	Time	Temp	Notes	Initials

Temperature Log

Title:	Equipment:
Contents:	
Temp. Range:	

Date	Time	Temp	Notes	Initials

Temperature Log

Title:	Equipment:
Contents:	
Temp. Range:	

Date	Time	Temp	Notes	Initials

Temperature Log

Title:	Equipment:
Contents:	
Temp. Range:	

Date	Time	Temp	Notes	Initials

Temperature Log

Title:	Equipment:
Contents:	
Temp. Range:	

Date	Time	Temp	Notes	Initials

Temperature Log

Title:	Equipment:
Contents:	
Temp. Range:	

Date	Time	Temp	Notes	Initials

Temperature Log

Title:				Equipment:
Contents:				
Temp. Range:				
Date	Time	Temp	Notes	Initials

Temperature Log

Title:	Equipment:
Contents:	
Temp. Range:	

Date	Time	Temp	Notes	Initials

Temperature Log

Title:	Equipment:
Contents:	
Temp. Range:	

Date	Time	Temp	Notes	Initials

Temperature Log

Title:	Equipment:
Contents:	
Temp. Range:	

Date	Time	Temp	Notes	Initials

Temperature Log

Title:	Equipment:
Contents:	
Temp. Range:	

Date	Time	Temp	Notes	Initials

Temperature Log

Title:	Equipment:
Contents:	
Temp. Range:	

Date	Time	Temp	Notes	Initials

Temperature Log

Title:			Equipment:	
Contents:				
Temp. Range:				
Date	Time	Temp	Notes	Initials

Temperature Log

Title:	Equipment:
Contents:	
Temp. Range:	

Date	Time	Temp	Notes	Initials

Temperature Log

Title:	Equipment:
Contents:	
Temp. Range:	

Date	Time	Temp	Notes	Initials

Temperature Log

Title:	Equipment:
Contents:	
Temp. Range:	

Date	Time	Temp	Notes	Initials

Temperature Log

Title:	Equipment:
Contents:	
Temp. Range:	

Date	Time	Temp	Notes	Initials

Temperature Log

Title:	Equipment:
Contents:	
Temp. Range:	

Date	Time	Temp	Notes	Initials

Temperature Log

Title:	Equipment:
Contents:	
Temp. Range:	

Date	Time	Temp	Notes	Initials

Temperature Log

Title:	Equipment:
Contents:	
Temp. Range:	

Date	Time	Temp	Notes	Initials

Temperature Log

Title:	Equipment:
Contents:	
Temp. Range:	

Date	Time	Temp	Notes	Initials

Temperature Log

Title:	Equipment:
Contents:	
Temp. Range:	

Date	Time	Temp	Notes	Initials

Temperature Log

Title:	Equipment:
Contents:	
Temp. Range:	

Date	Time	Temp	Notes	Initials

Made in the USA
Monee, IL
14 May 2021

68502053R00059